# WORKBOOK FOR

A
MIDSUMMER
NIGHT'S
DREAM

THE GRAPHIC NOVEL

※ HEINLE
CENGAGE Learning·

Australia • Brazil • Japan • Korea • Mexico • Singapore • Spain • United Kingdom • United States

**Workbook for A Midsummer Night's Dream:
The Graphic Novel**

Publisher: Sherrise Roehr

Associate Development Editor: Cécile Engeln

Director of U.S. Marketing: Jim McDonough

Director of Content Production: Michael Burggren

Associate Content Project Manager:
    Mark Rzeszutek

Character Design and Artwork: Jason Candy and
    Kat Nicholson

Lettering: Jim Campbell

Associate Editor: Joe Sutliff Sanders

Design and Layout: Jenny Placentino

Compositor: MPS Limited, a Macmillan Company

Cover Design: Gina Petti, Rotunda Design

For product information and technology assistance, contact us at
Cengage Learning Customer & Sales support, 1-800-354-9706
For permission to use material from this text or product,
submit all requests online at **www.cengage.com/permissions**
Further permissions questions can be e-mailed to
**permissionrequest@cengage.com**

ISBN 13: 978-1-111-83846-1

ISBN 10: 1-111-83846-1

**Heinle**
20 Channel Center Street
Boston, MA 02210
USA

Cengage Learning is a leading provider of customised learning solutions with office locations around the globe, including Singapore, the United Kingdom, Australia, Mexico, Brazil and Japan. Locate our local office at:
**international.cengage.com/region**

Cengage Learning products are represented in Canada by Nelson Education, Ltd.

Visit Heinle online at **elt.heinle.com**

Visit our corporate website at **www.cengage.com**

Printed in the United States of America
1 2 3 4 5 6 7 8 9 10 14 13 12 11

# CONTENTS

# Before You Read
## Worksheet 1 – Know Your Shakespeare

**A.** Choose the best answer to each question by circling the letter of the correct answer.

1. William Shakespeare was born in _____.
   **a.** London     **b.** Gloucester     **c.** Stratford-upon-Avon     **d.** Salisbury

2. His father was _____.
   **a.** a wealthy nobleman     **b.** a farmer     **c.** very poor     **d.** a tradesman

3. Shakespeare's wife's name was _____.
   **a.** Mary     **b.** Elizabeth     **c.** Anne     **d.** Helen

4. Shakespeare wrote a total of _____ plays.
   **a.** 24     **b.** 38     **c.** 42     **d.** 16

5. He had three children, _____.
   **a.** two boys and a girl     **b.** all girls     **c.** all boys     **d.** two girls and a boy

6. Shakespeare lived in Elizabethan England. This means he lived_____.
   **a.** when Elizabeth was a popular name
   **b.** when Elizabeth I was Queen
   **c.** in the time of Queen Elizabeth II
   **d.** in an area of England called Elizabeth

Now read about Shakespeare on pp. 139–140 and find out if you were right.

**B.** Complete the timeline of Shakespeare's life.

| Approximate Date | What Happened? |
|---|---|
| 1564 | |
| 1582 | *He married . . .* |
| 1583–1585 | |
| 1587 | |
| 1590–1613 | |
| 1616 | |
| 1670 | |

**C.** Circle the titles of the plays that were written by Shakespeare

| | | | |
|---|---|---|---|
| *The Tempest* | *The White Devil* | *King Lear* | *The Merchant of Venice* |
| *Tamburlaine* | *Othello* | *Macbeth* | *A Midsummer Night's Dream* |

**D.** Can you name any other Shakespeare plays? Make a list.

# Before You Read

## Worksheet 2 – The Story

**A.** Read the first two columns of "History of A Midsummer Night's Dream" on p. 141. Circle true or false. If the statement is false, make it true and write it on the lines.

1. *A Midsummer Night's Dream* was written for a wedding.        True        False

   _____

   _____

2. Shakespeare wrote *A Midsummer Night's Dream* in 1600.        True        False

   _____

   _____

3. Elizabeth I was queen of England when *A Midsummer Night's Dream* was written.        True        False

   _____

   _____

4. Today, *A Midsummer Night's Dream* is still popular.        True        False

   _____

   _____

**B.** Read the section titled "Time and Place" in "History of A Midsummer Night's Dream" on p. 141. Fill in the blanks with the correct dates and years.

1. When the play was written, people thought the summer solstice was on _____.
2. On today's calendars, the summer solstice is on _____.
3. We celebrate the winter solstice on _____.
4. Part of the play happens on _____.
5. The real Theseus lived in Greece in _____.

**C.** Read the items below. Check each item that is from *A Midsummer Night's Dream*.

1. _____ A father wants his daughter to marry someone she doesn't love.
2. _____ There are characters named Romeo and Juliet.
3. _____ An arrow is shot at a queen.
4. _____ James I becomes king of England.
5. _____ There's a summer solstice celebration.
6. _____ There is a character named Theseus.
7. _____ Some young couples are found in a forest.
8. _____ People come from Athens, Greece.

Name: _____

**A.** Read the section titled "Sources" in "History of A Midsummer Night's Dream" on p. 142. Then read each item below and write the letter(s) of the source(s) that it came from.

1. _____ bad weather caused by an argument between Titania and Oberon
2. _____ the story of Theseus and Hippolyta
3. _____ the story of Pyramus and Thisbe
4. _____ the names Robin Goodfellow and Hobgoblin
5. _____ the names Philostrate and Egeus
6. _____ a character's head turning into a donkey's head

    **a.** *Metamorphoses*
    **b.** *Canterbury Tales*
    **c.** *The Discoverie of Witchcraft*
    **d.** *Transformations of Lucius or The Golden Ass*

**B.** Read "Shakespeare's Globe" on p. 143. Label the parts of the theater with the words from the box.

| galleries | stage | thatched roof | yard |
|---|---|---|---|

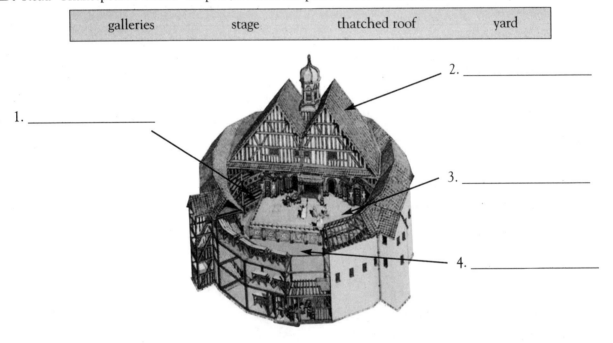

1. _____

2. _____

3. _____

4. _____

**C.** Complete the chart about the three Globe Theaters. Include information about when each was built, how and why each closed, how many people each could hold, and other important information.

|  | **The Globe** | **The Second Globe** | **The New Globe** |
|---|---|---|---|
| When was it built/moved? |  |  |  |
| When was it closed? |  |  | — |
| Why was it closed? |  |  | — |
| How many people could/can it hold? |  | — |  |

Name: _____

**A.** Shakespeare wrote three different kinds of plays: comedies, tragedies, and histories. Match the definitions below with the kind of play by writing the letter of the correct definition.

    **1.** _____ comedy        **a.** a serious play with a sad ending

    **2.** _____ tragedy        **b.** a play based on the life of an English king

    **3.** _____ history        **c.** a lighthearted play with a happy ending

**B.** A **play** is organized into acts and scenes. An **act** is one of the main parts into which a play is divided; it can contain several scenes. A **scene** is a series of events that occur in the same place.

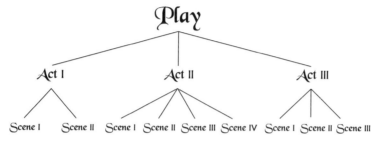

Look at the Contents for *A Midsummer Night's Dream* on p. 3. How many acts does *A Midsummer Night's Dream* have? _____

**C.** Match the parts of a play with their definitions by writing the letter of the correct definition.

    **1.** _____ plot        **a.** the words that the characters say

    **2.** _____ prologue        **b.** the story of a play

    **3.** _____ dialogue        **c.** the most exciting part of a play

    **4.** _____ climax        **d.** where a play takes place

    **5.** _____ stage directions        **e.** a speech that introduces a play

    **6.** _____ setting        **f.** instructions for the actors in a play

**D.** Now match the types of characters with their descriptions.

    **1.** _____ character        **a.** the most important person in a play

    **2.** _____ protagonist        **b.** the evil, bad person in a play

    **3.** _____ chorus        **c.** a person in the play

    **4.** _____ villain        **d.** a person who introduces the story in a play

**E.** As you read *A Midsummer Night's Dream*, complete the chart below with examples of each term from the play.

| | |
|---|---|
| **protagonist(s)** | Puck |
| **setting(s)** | |
| **climax** | |
| **foreshadowing** | |

# Before You Read

## Worksheet 5 – Meet the Characters

Cut out the faces and then glue or tape them in the correct spaces below.

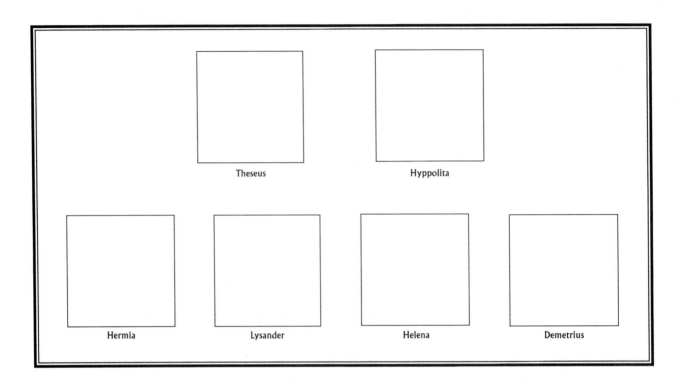

Theseus

Hyppolita

Hermia

Lysander

Helena

Demetrius

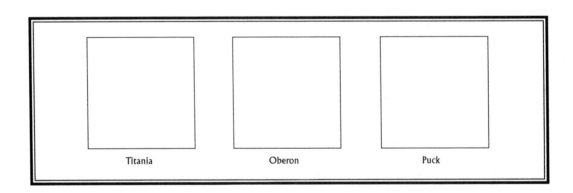

Titania

Oberon

Puck

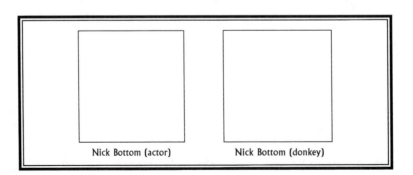

Nick Bottom (actor)

Nick Bottom (donkey)

# Before You Read

## Cutouts for Worksheet 5 – Meet the Characters

Cut out the faces. Then glue or tape them in the correct places on Worksheet 5.

Name: _____

# While You Read
## Worksheet 6 – Act I, Scene I, pp. 7–20

CD 1
Track 1

**A.** Read and listen to Act I, Scene I, pp. 7–14. Fill in the missing information.

1. The story opens in the _____ in Athens.

2. Theseus and Hippolyta's wedding celebration will take place in _____ days.

3. _____ is Hermia's father.

4. He has given permission to Hermia to marry _____ .

5. Hermia wants to marry _____ .

6. _____ is Demetrius's admirer.

**B.** Review Act I, Scene I, pp. 7–14. Complete the summary below using the words in the word bank.

| cast a spell | convent | disobey | execute | holy | lively |
|---|---|---|---|---|---|
| noble | nun | obey | point of view | refuses | |

*A Midsummer Night's Dream* is a story about love. In the story, a young woman named Hermia
**1.** _____ to marry Demetrius, the man that her father has chosen for her. Instead, she
loves another man named Lysander. Lysander is as **2.** _____ and rich as Demetrius.
Hermia's father thinks that Lysander has **3.** _____ on his daughter, tricking her into
loving him. Hermia's father is very angry with her, and he says that he will **4.** _____
her if she continues to **5.** _____ him. Hermia asks Theseus, the Duke of Athens, what
will happen to her if she doesn't **6.** _____ her father. Theseus asks Hermia to try to
understand her father's **7.** _____. Theseus explains that Hermia's only other choice is to
live a **8.** _____ life in a **9.** _____. However, Theseus doesn't think that
Hermia would be happy as a **10.** _____ because she is such a **11.** _____
young woman.

CD 1
Track 2

**C.** Read and listen to Act I, Scene II, pp. 15–20. Circle true or false. If the statement is false, make it true
and write it on the lines.

1. Lysander wants to go to his aunt's home because Athenian laws don't apply there.　　True　　False

_____

_____

2. Hermia thinks it's her fault that Demetrius loves her.　　True　　False

_____

_____

3. Demetrius and Helena used to be in a relationship together.　　True　　False

_____

_____

4. Hermia and Lysander plan to sneak out of Athens tonight.　　True　　False

_____

_____

## While You Read

## Worksheet 6 – Act I, Scene I (Continued)

**D.** Read Helena's lines from Act I, Scene II, p. 20. What has happened to her to make her say these things? Write your answer.

"Love is so blind. It has no judgment or taste. Love is so unfair. It lies and breaks its promises."

_____

_____

_____

**E.** Review Act I, Scene I. Answer the questions.

**1.** According to Egeus, what did Lysander do to trick Hermia into loving him?

_____

_____

_____

**2.** Lysander says that things never run smoothly in stories of love. What examples does he give?

_____

_____

_____

**3.** Does Hermia like Helena? How do you know?

_____

_____

_____

**4.** What does Helena decide to do at the end of Act I? Why?

_____

_____

_____

**5.** Think of a movie, book, or play about a love that doesn't run smoothly. What is the title? What problems does the couple have?

_____

_____

_____

Name: _____

# While You Read
## Worksheet 7 – Act I, Scene II, pp. 21–26

**CD 1**
**Track 3**

**A.** Read and listen to Act I, Scene II, pp. 21–26. Answer the questions.

  **1.** Where does this scene take place?

    _____

    _____

  **2.** What play are the actors going to perform?

    _____

    _____

  **3.** Where are they going to perform the play?

    _____

    _____

  **4.** Why does Nick Bottom want to play all the characters?

    _____

    _____

  **5.** Peter Quince says to Nick Bottom, "Pyramus is a very handsome man. He is very good-looking. So, you have to be Pyramus!" Why does he say this?

    _____

    _____

  **6.** Where and when are the actors going to rehearse?

    _____

    _____

**B.** Match each actor with the character he will play.

  **1.** _____ Nick Bottom          **a.** Thisbe's mother
  **2.** _____ Francis Flute          **b.** Thisbe
  **3.** _____ Robin Starveling     **c.** Thisbe's father
  **4.** _____ Tom Snout           **d.** the lion
  **5.** _____ Peter Quince         **e.** Pyramus's father
  **6.** _____ Snug                **f.** Pyramus

**C.** Circle the word or phrase that completes each sentence.

  **1.** In the setting of this play, people could <u>shock/hang</u> if they did something wrong.
  **2.** Before you can perform in a play, you have to learn your <u>lines/characters</u>.
  **3.** Some actors <u>rehearse/perform</u> a play for several weeks before anyone sees the play.
  **4.** Many people become actors because they like to <u>rehearse/perform</u> in front of people.
  **5.** A <u>dove/tyrant</u> is a cruel leader.
  **6.** A <u>dove/tyrant</u> is a kind of bird.
  **7.** The <u>audience/cast</u> of a play is made up of actors.
  **8.** A play is performed for an <u>audience/cast</u>.

Name: _____

# While You Read

## Worksheet 8 – Act II, Scene I, pp. 27–34

CD 1
Track 4

**A.** Read and listen to Act II, Scene I, pp. 27–34. Then close your book. Read each sentence below and circle the character who said it.

| | | | |
|---|---|---|---|
| 1. "Where are you going, spirit?" | Puck | Fairy |
| 2. "I serve the fairy queen, keeping everything beautiful and green." | Puck | Fairy |
| 3. "I make her fairy rings clean and neat." | Puck | Fairy |
| 4. "That's me all right! The happy traveler of the night." | Puck | Fairy |
| 5. "How can you talk to me about Hippolyta?" | Titania | Oberon |
| 6. "All I want is the little boy to be my page." | Titania | Oberon |
| 7. "I am raising him. I will not leave him!" | Titania | Oberon |
| 8. "Come here, Puck." | Titania | Oberon |

**B.** Match the vocabulary words and phrases with their definitions.

1. _____ crop
2. _____ relationship
3. _____ out of sight
4. _____ disguise
5. _____ jealous
6. _____ pay for something

a. unable to be seen by anyone else
b. alter your appearance so that people will not recognize you
c. plants such as wheat and potatoes that are grown in large quantities for food
d. deal with the consequences of something you've done
e. a close friendship between two people
f. feeling angry or bitter because you do not have something that someone else has

**C.** Answer the questions.

1. What are Puck's other names?

_____

_____

2. What is Puck known for?

_____

_____

3. What does Oberon want from Titania?

_____

_____

4. Why won't she give it to him?

_____

_____

# While You Read
## Worksheet 9 – Act II, Scene I, pp. 35–41

CD 1
Track 5

**A.** Read and listen to Act II, Scene I, pp. 35–41. Put the events in the order that they occur.

1. _____          a. Oberon asks Puck to bring the flower to him.
2. _____          b. Puck brings the flower to Oberon.
3. _____          c. Oberon asks Puck to put the juice of the flower on Demetrius's eyelids.
4. _____          d. Oberon hears someone coming.
5. _____          e. Oberon decides to help Helena.
6. _____          f. Oberon tells Puck about a special flower.
7. _____          g. Oberon listens to Helena and Demetrius.

**B.** Complete the summary. Fill in the blanks with the words from the word bank.

| | | | | | | |
|---|---|---|---|---|---|---|
| arrow | Athenians | attracts | Cupid | eyelids | invisible | lovesick |
| magnet | rejects | spell | target | | | |

Oberon and Puck are in the woods after Oberon's conversation with Titania. Oberon reminds Puck
of the time he saw **1.** _____ shoot a(n) **2.** _____ at a queen to make her fall in love with
someone. Cupid missed his **3.** _____ and shot a flower instead. Oberon wants Puck to get that
flower. Oberon wants to squeeze its juice onto Titania's **4.** _____ while she's sleeping. It will make
her fall in love with the first person she sees when she wakes up. Oberon will break the **5.** _____
when Titania gives him what she wants.

After Puck leaves to get the flower, Oberon hears two **6.** _____ in the woods—Demetrius and
Helena. He makes himself **7.** _____ so he can listen to them. He learns that Helena is following
Demetrius because she is **8.** _____. She explains that Demetrius **9.** _____ her like a
**10.** _____. But Demetrius **11.** _____ Helena and walks away. Then, Puck returns with
the flower.

**C.** Answer the questions.

1. Why does Oberon want Titania to fall in love with something horrible?

    _____

    _____

2. Why are Demetrius and Helena in the woods?

    _____

    _____

3. What time of day is it? What words in the play tell you what time of day it is?

    _____

    _____

4. Why do you think Oberon wants to help Helena?

    _____

    _____

# While You Read
## Worksheet 10 – Act II, Scene II, pp. 42–53

CD 1
Track 6

**A.** Read and listen to Act II, Scene II, pp. 42–53. Complete each sentence with the correct name. You will not use all the names. You will use some names more than once.

| Helena | Hermia | Demetrius | Lysander | fairies | Oberon | Titania |

1. The _____ sing Titania to sleep.
2. _____ puts flower juice on Titania's eyelids.
3. _____ and _____ are walking in the woods when they decide to stop and sleep.
4. Puck puts flower juice on _____'s eyelids.
5. Helena is tired from fighting with _____.
6. _____ falls off a cliff and finds _____. She doesn't know if he's alive or dead.
7. _____ wakes up and falls in love with Helena.
8. _____ wakes up and finds that Lysander is gone.

**B.** Write each word next to its definition.

| charm | compete | magic | nightmare |

1. _____: a very frightening dream
2. _____: a magical force that may change a person or cause them to act differently
3. _____: try to get something for yourself and stop someone else from getting it
4. _____: the power to use supernatural forces to make impossible things happen

**C.** Answer the questions. Write three sentences to describe the events in each illustration. Include what happened before and after each event in your descriptions.

1.
_____
_____
_____
_____
_____
_____
_____

2.
_____
_____
_____
_____
_____
_____
_____
_____
_____
_____
_____

# While You Read

## Worksheet 11 – Act III, Scene I, pp. 54–63

**A.** Read and listen to Act III, Scene I, pp. 54–63. Circle true or false. If a statement is false, make it true.

1. The actors are in the woods to rehearse their play.                                              True     False

_____

_____

2. Oberon is sleeping nearby.                                              True     False

_____

_____

3. Peter Quince wants to change some things in the play.                                              True     False

_____

_____

4. The actors make several mistakes while they're rehearsing.                                              True     False

_____

_____

5. Puck thinks Bottom is clever.                                              True     False

_____

_____

6. Puck runs away from the other actors.                                              True     False

_____

_____

7. Titania gets angry when Puck wakes her up with his singing.                                              True     False

_____

_____

8. Titania's fairies think Bottom is handsome and smart.                                              True     False

_____

_____

**B.** Complete the sentences by using the words in the word bank.

| angel | bow | courtesy | introductions | monster | nest | odious | reason |
|-------|-----|----------|---------------|---------|------|--------|--------|

1. Bottom wants to write _____ to explain different characters in the play to the audience.

2. Puck seems to think Bottom is _____. That's why he plays a trick on him.

3. When the actors see Bottom, they think he is a(n) _____.

4. When Titania hears Bottom singing, she thinks he sounds like a(n) _____.

5. Titania wants the fairies to show _____ to her new love.

6. Titania also wants the fairies to _____ to Bottom to show their respect.

7. The word _____ has two meanings. It is a fact or situation which explains why something happens. It is also the ability to think and make sensible judgments.

8. Titania asks her fairies to bring Bottom to her _____ to sleep.

Name: _____

CD 1
Track 8

**A.** Read and listen to Act III, Scene II, pp. 64–89. Put the events in the order that they occur.

1. _____         **a.** Demetrius wakes from his nap, sees Helena, and falls in love with her.

2. _____         **b.** Puck tells Oberon that Titania is in love with a monster.

3. _____         **c.** Puck uses the juice of the other flower to break the spell on Lysander.

4. _____         **d.** The four Athenians fall asleep not knowing that they're all next to each other.

5. _____         **e.** Hermia runs off, but Demetrius is tired, so he takes a nap.

6. _____         **f.** Hermia and Demetrius appear and Puck sees that something has gone wrong—it's the right woman, but the wrong man.

7. _____         **g.** Oberon puts juice on Demetrius's eyes.

8. _____         **h.** Puck creates fog and leads Lysander and Demetrius away from each other.

9. _____         **i.** Lysander and Demetrius begin to fight over Helena.

**B.** Write each word next to its definition.

| | | | | |
|---|---|---|---|---|
| bow | coward | dwarf | fog | in on something |
| murder | murderer | self-respect | vicious | vow |

1. _____: tiny drops of water in the air which form a thick cloud and make it difficult to see things

2. _____: someone who is easily frightened and avoids dangerous or difficult situations

3. _____: violent and cruel

4. _____: a feeling of confidence and pride in your own ability and worth

5. _____: a weapon for shooting arrows that consists of a long piece of curved wood with a string attached to both its ends

6. _____: a serious promise or decision to do a particular thing

7. _____: participating or having knowledge about what is going on

8. _____: to commit the crime of killing someone deliberately

9. _____: in children's stories, an imaginary creature that is like a small man; these men often have magical powers

10. _____: a person who commits the crime of killing someone

**C.** There is a lot of romantic confusion in the play. Some of it happens without magic, and some of it happens because of magic. Check the correct column for each situation below.

| | With magic | Without magic |
|---|---|---|
| 1. Hermia loves Lysander | | |
| 2. Helena loves Demetrius | | |
| 3. Demetrius loves Hermia | | |
| 4. Demetrius loves Helena | | |
| 5. Lysander loves Helena | | |
| 6. Lysander loves Hermia | | |
| 7. Titania loves Bottom | | |

## While You Read

**D.** Read each quote below and identify the character who says it.

| Quote | Speaker |
|---|---|
| 1. "I wonder what awful thing she saw and fell in love with." | |
| 2. ". . . while he was in there, I gave him a donkey head to wear." | |
| 3. "Did you put the juice in the eyes of the man from Athens?" | |
| 4. "Lysander wouldn't just leave me while I was sleeping." | |
| 5. "You murdered him!" | |
| 6. "I didn't murder him." | |
| 7. "You have used the juice on the wrong man!" | |
| 8. "Look at Helena when you wake; then, for her, your heart will ache." | |
| 9. "My what fools these humans are." | |
| 10. "You all want to make fun of me!" | |
| 11. "Demetrius, I know you love Hermia. You can have her." | |
| 12. "Does he have a higher opinion of you because I am short?" | |

**E.** Answer the questions.

1. How does Puck feel about the fact that he used the magic flower on the wrong Athenian? Find evidence in the scene to support your answer.

   _____
   _____
   _____
   _____

2. How does Oberon feel about it? Find evidence in the scene to support your answer.

   _____
   _____
   _____
   _____

3. Why does Helena call Demetrius and Hermia "snake"?

   _____
   _____
   _____
   _____

4. Puck says, "What a joke we would have played if two men love the same fair maid." What does he not realize?

   _____
   _____
   _____
   _____

Name: _____

CD 2
Track 2-3

**A.** Read and listen to Act IV, Scene I and Act IV, Scene II, pp. 90–107. Fill in the missing information.

1. Titania wants to put _____ on Bottom's head.

2. Bottom wants Peaseblossom to _____ his head.

3. He wants Cobweb to bring him some _____.

4. Bottom wants to eat some _____, _____, _____, or _____.

5. Oberon tells Puck that he saw Titania in the forest earlier, and she gave him the _____.

6. Puck removes Bottom's donkey head, and Oberon removes the _____ from Titania.

7. Theseus and Hippolyta find the couples while they are out _____.

8. When Bottom and the other Athenians wake up, they each think they had a _____.

**B.** Circle the word or phrase that completes each sentence.

1. During most of the play, there is a lot of **jealousy / performance** between Demetrius and Lysander.

2. Demetrius was **hazy / engaged** to Helena in the past.

3. Because of the magic spell, Titania **adores / grates** Bottom.

4. Flute likes Bottom's voice. He doesn't think it **adores / grates**.

5. Without Bottom, there will be no **performance / gamekeeper**.

**C.** Write three sentences to describe the events in each illustration. Include what happened before and after each event in your descriptions.

1.

_____
_____
_____
_____
_____
_____

2.

_____
_____
_____
_____
_____
_____
_____
_____
_____
_____

# While You Read
## Worksheet 14 – Act V, Scene I, pp. 108–112

CD 2
Track 4

**A.** Read and listen to Act V, Scene I, pp. 108–112. Then read each quote below and write the name of the character who says it.

| Quote | Speaker |
|---|---|
| **1.** "Lovers and crazy people have wild imaginations." | |
| **2.** "But they're all saying the same story. They couldn't have all had the same dream." | |
| **3.** "They are not very good, and they have had to work hard to memorize their lines." | |
| **4.** "I want to see the play. They will do their best." | |
| **5.** "I don't like to see people make fools of themselves." | |
| **6.** "Their mistakes will be funny; and, if hard work doesn't make them good, we will respect them for trying." | |

**B.** Replace the underlined words and phrases with the correct vocabulary words from the box.

| entertainment | fairy tales | sincere | supernatural force |
|---|---|---|---|

**1.** _____ Theseus doesn't believe what the young couples have told them about their evening in the forest. He thinks they're telling <u>silly stories</u>.

**2.** _____ He says that lovers think some <u>magic</u> makes good things happen for them.

**3.** _____ Theseus appreciates it when people are <u>honest</u>, even if they are nervous and have trouble saying what they mean.

**4.** _____ Theseus, Hippolyta, and the young couples go into the theater to watch the <u>show</u>.

**C.** Philostrate gives Theseus a list of entertainment to choose from. Match each play with Theseus' reaction to it.

**1.** _____ Hercules's Battle with the Centaurs, to the Tune of a Harp

**2.** _____ The Death of Orpheus, Killed by Drunken Woman

**3.** _____ The Destruction of Learning

**4.** _____ Pyramus and Thisbe: a Boring and Brief Tragic Comedy

**a.** "Too serious for a wedding."

**b.** "Funny and tragice? Boring and brief? How can that be? What is it?"

**c.** "I have already told that story to Hippolyta."

**d.** "I saw that when I returned from conquering the city of Thebes."

# While You Read

## Worksheet 15 – Act V, Scene I, pp. 113–132

CD 2
Track 5

**A.** Read and listen to Act V, Scene I, pp. 113–127. Then read the items below and circle the correct answers.

1. The play *Pyramus and Thisbe* is meant to be a _____.

   a. comedy     b. tragedy     c. history

2. Because of the way the actors perform *Pyramus and Thisbe*, the play is _____.

   a. funny     b. sad     c. historic

3. The actor with the _____ is playing the crescent moon.

   a. wall     b. cape     c. lantern

4. The actors end the play with _____.

   a. a speech     b. a story     c. a dance

**B.** Answer the questions.

1. Bottom makes a lot of mistakes in *Pyramus and Thisbe*. Describe three mistakes that he makes.

   _____

   _____

   _____

2. What does the audience think of the play *Pyramus and Thisbe*? Find three details in the play to support your answer.

   _____

   _____

   _____

CD 2
Track 6

**C.** Read and listen to Act V, Scene I, pp. 128–132. Compare Quince's introduction to the play on p. 113, to Puck's speech on p. 132. How are they similar? How are they different? Complete the Venn diagram.

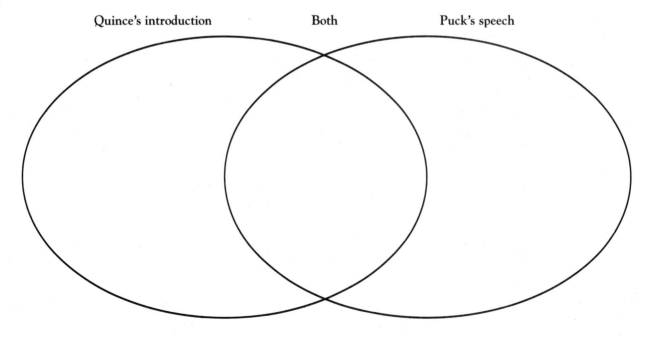

Quince's introduction        Both        Puck's speech

## After You Read
## Worksheet 16 – Matching Quotes

Cut out all the cards and match each quote to the character who said it.

| | |
|---|---|
| "If she does not marry Demetrius, I will have her executed." | **Theseus** |
| "All I want is the little boy to be my page." | **Hippolyta** |
| "I don't believe any of these fairy tales." | **Hermia** |
| "Let's watch from afar. My, what fools these humans are!" | **Helena** |
| "This is how vines wrap around trees. How I love you! How I adore you!" | **Lysander** |
| "I can be anything—even a tyrant king, like Hercules." | **Demetrius** |
| "Teach me how to be like you so Demetrius will love me." | **Egeus** |

## After You Read

### Worksheet 16 – Matching Quotes (Continued)

| | |
|---|---|
| "Scratch my head, Peaseblossom." | **Philostrate** |
| "If you follow me, I may have to hurt you." | **Titania** |
| "Four days will pass quickly. Then we will be married." | **Oberon** |
| "I would rather be a nun than marry someone I do not love." | **Puck** |
| "I cried with laughter when I saw it being rehearsed." | **Bottom as a donkey** |
| "Sneak out tomorrow night and meet me in the forest." | **Peter Quince** |
| "Ladies and gentlemen, on with the show! Here are some things you need to know." | **Bottom** |

# After You Read
## Worksheet 17 – Characters and Adjectives

Fill in the boxes with adjectives that describe the characters. You can use some adjectives more than once, and you don't need to use them all.

Put an asterisk (*) next to adjectives that describe the characters after they have been affected by magic.

| | | |
|---|---|---|
| aggressive | desperate | lacking confidence |
| brave | disloyal (to the person he/she loves) | loyal (to the person he/she loves) |
| confident | light-haired | noble |
| cruel | in love | rich |
| dark-haired | jealous | short |

| | |
|---|---|
| | **Hermia** |
| | **Lysander** |
| | **Helena** |
| | **Demetrius** |

# After You Read

## Worksheet 18 – Star-crossed Lovers

In Act I, Scene I, we learn that Hermia and Lysander are forbidden to marry. This situation is similar to the conflict in *Pyramus and Thisbe*. Use the chart below to compare the two stories.

| Question: | Lysander and Hermia | Pyramus and Thisbe |
|---|---|---|
| Who is against their marriage and why? | | |
| What do they do to try to be together? | | |
| Does their plan work? | | |
| What is the outcome? | | |
| What is the main reason for this outcome? | | |

# After You Read
## Worksheet 19 – Journal Entries

Choose a character. Then choose a scene. Imagine you are the character. Write your thoughts and feelings in a journal entry on a separate sheet of paper.

### Hermia

1. Act I, Scene I: Egeus forbids Hermia to marry Lysander. She has four days to decide whether she wants to become a nun, marry Demetrius, or be executed.

2. Act IV, Scene I: Theseus announces that Hermia will marry Lysander and Helena will marry Demetrius.

### Helena

1. Act II, Scene I: Helena is chasing Demetrius in the woods.

2. Act III, Scene II: Lysander and Demetrius both seem to be in love with Helena.

### Demetrius

1. Act I, Scene I: Egeus wants Hermia to marry Demetrius, but Hermia wants to marry Lysander.

2. Act II, Scene I: Helena is chasing Demetrius in the woods.

### Lysander

1. Act I, Scene I: Lysander wants to marry Hermia, but she is supposed to marry Demetrius.

2. Act III, Scene II: Lysander discovers that he is in love with Helena and not in love with Hermia anymore.

### Bottom

1. Act I, Scene II: Bottom finds out he is going to play Pyramus.

2. Act IV, Scene I: Bottom wakes up in the forest with the fairies.

### Puck

1. Act III, Scene I: Puck gives Bottom a donkey's head.

2. Act III, Scene II: Puck realizes that he put the flower juice in the wrong man's eyes.

Name: _____

## After You Read

In *A Midsummer Night's Dream*, Shakespeare brings three different worlds together and three different plots. First, the Athenians are in a plot revolving around love, marriage, and finding the perfect partner. The second world is that of the actors staging a story of tragic love. Finally, there is the fairy world, with its troubled King Oberon and Queen Titania. The diagram below shows how Shakespeare structures and interweaves the three worlds into one story. Fill in the squares, briefly describing the events that take place. The first one is done for you.

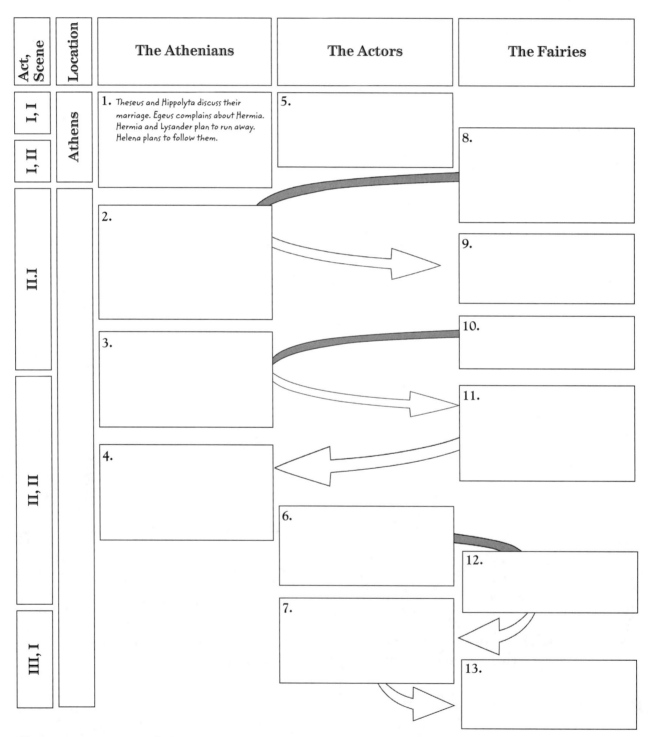

Name: _____

# Worksheet 20 – The Different Worlds in *A Midsummer Night's Dream*

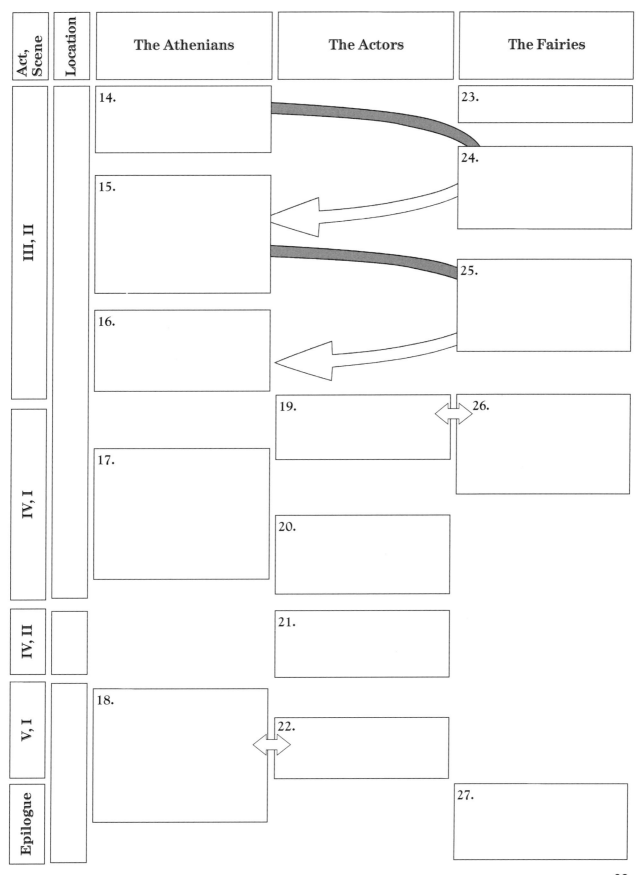

| Act, Scene | Location | The Athenians | The Actors | The Fairies |
|---|---|---|---|---|
| III, II | | 14. | | 23. |
| | | 15. | | 24. |
| | | 16. | | 25. |
| IV, I | | 17. | 19. | 26. |
| | | | 20. | |
| IV, II | | | 21. | |
| V, I | | 18. | 22. | |
| Epilogue | | | | 27. |

# After You Read
## Crossword Puzzle

Use the clues to complete the crossword puzzle.

**Across**

   3. The part played by Snout, separating the lovers in the actors' play
   6. Theseus's fiancé
   8. Theseus hunts with these
  10. The fairy queen
  11. Theseus is the duke of this
  13. The type of head put on Bottom by Puck
  14. The boy whom Hermia's father wants her to marry
  16. The leader of the acting group: Peter _____

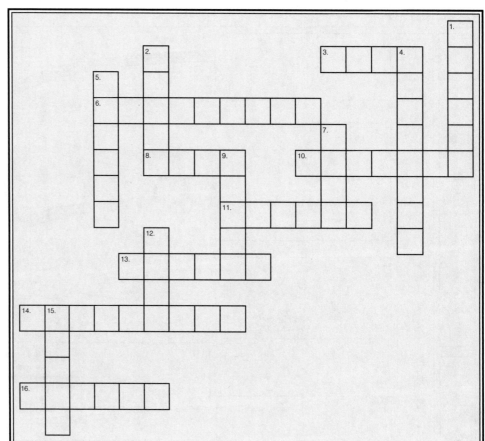

**Down**

   1. Hermia's friend and occasional love rival
   2. The god whose arrow hit the flower
   4. Hermia's true love
   5. The play performed for Theseus: *Pyramus* and _____
   7. Snug's role in the actors' play
   9. What Hermia dreams about
  12. In Act I, Scene I, how many days until the wedding?
  15. Hermia's father